Praise

Do we really need another leadership book? With *Apples and Oranges on Your Team*, it's a resounding, *yes*! This delightful collection of parables and imagery offers life and leadership lessons in a refreshing storytelling format. Prepare to increase your emotional intelligence and leadership, one entertaining short story at a time.

—Kristin A. Sherry, creator of the YouMap® Career Profile and Amazon international bestselling author of *YouMap, Maximize365,* and *Your Team Loves Mondays… Right?*

Steve inspires through impactful storytelling that tugs at your heart, makes you think and reflect. You are in for a joyous ride.

—Parul Banka, speaker, story coach, and author of *My Cancer Journey: A Rendezvous with Myself.*

Several words come to mind when reading *Apples and Oranges on Your Team*: leadership, enjoyment, personal growth, and team enhancement—a must-read for leaders who aspire to greatness.

—Renee Vidor, founder of *The Winner's Circle* and author of *Measuring Up: How to WIN in a World of Comparison.*

Steve Sullivan is a masterful storyteller and an efficient writer who inspires leaders and future leaders to grow.

—Anna Sabino, bestselling author of *Your Creative Career,* and branding and visibility coach.

For years, Steve Sullivan has been inspiring people around the world with his #StorySaturday series. Now you can learn from this master storyteller as he shares insightful stories in *Apples and Oranges on Your Team.* Enjoy!

—Andy Kaufman, speaker, author, executive coach, and host of the *People and Projects Podcast.*

Steve Sullivan is a leader's leader. Steve beautifully understands the dynamics of teams and how to connect with people at a core level to promote their inner greatness. When you read *Apples and Oranges on Your Team,* you'll understand why. I intentionally encourage you to pick up a copy of this book today. Bring more positivity and connection to your team with these stories.

—Brian Sexton, author of *People Buy from People* and host of *The Intentional Encourager Podcast.*

Steve lives by the values he teaches. His insight and experience will guide you in your life. His creative storytelling is truly relatable in a way that will help you grow personally and professionally.

> —Jacqueline Way, Top 100 TEDx speaker and founder of #365give and #Do1Give Day.

The stories Steve shares in this book challenge you as a leader.

> —Marlo Higgins, author of *The Making of a Maverick* and creator of Maverick ROI High-Performance System.

APPLES AND ORANGES ON YOUR TEAM

BITE-SIZE STORIES FOR LIFE-GIVING LEADERSHIP

STEVEN LEE SULLIVAN

Published by Author Academy Elite
P.O. Box 43, Powell, OH 43065
www.AuthorAcademyElite.com

Identifiers:

Library of Congress Control Number: 2021914712

ISBN: 978-1-64746-861-3 (paperback)
ISBN: 978-1-64746-862-0 (hardback)
ISBN: 978-1-64746-863-7 (ebook)

Available in paperback, hardback, e-book, and audiobook

Dedication

This book is a tribute to the example of my parents, Dr. Leonard Sullivan, MD, and Betty Sullivan, PhD, and their incredible legacy of leadership.

My father was a man known through the lives he touched. He blessed and prayed over each new infant born into his practice. On his wall hangs a painting by a single mother who, after she cleaned up her life, he helped regain custody of her children. On another occasion, he camped for three days in a child's hospital room to help pull a boy through an adverse reaction. In all his actions, he exemplified compassion for the sick and needy.

My mother thrives in leading, never afraid to fill a role, whether a professional position in the School of Nursing at Wichita State University or as a volunteer supporting charity work or as the president of the National Airstream

Club. Her compassion extended to working with abused women, often hosting support groups. As a woman in her eighties, she continues to lead where needed as she remains active in leadership roles for multiple groups.

Thank you, Dad and Mom, for your legacy; I would not be the man I am today without it.

Contents

Acknowledgments

Thank you to my writing partner *Mario Castelli,* who helped me refine my craft of writing stories and believed in them to rescue several from the trash bin.

Thank you to my editors and The Guild for their assistance during the final stage of the manuscript. My editors were instructors who helped me mold my book like clay into a beautiful vase. Thank you to my structure editor, *Emily (Mimi) Ann Velilla,* whose valuable feedback elevated this book to another level. I am grateful to my line editor *Jack Hempfling* who helped me add more details to the stories, and copy editor *Jill Armijo* for putting the finishing touches on the masterpiece.

Thank you, *Dave Carroll,* who encouraged and challenged me to keep writing these stories and not quit after a few.

I am thankful for the following people for their collaboration with these stories. They added valuable insights to each message. Their partnership became my motivation to write these stories.

I gratefully acknowledge *Mic De Fazio, Falguni Katira, Elizabeth Lim, Jared Wiese, Kristen Prewitt, April Hall, Randy Heller, Belinda Aramide, Jason Loye, Patrick Ward, Rachel Stuve, Martin Baumeister, Rob Deptford, Olivia Schmitt, Joseph Saheb Bakkhsh, Joy Abdullah, Kristin Sherry, Devina Kaur, Chantel Soumis, Anna Sabino, Doug Thompson, Michelle Rademacher, Lori Knudsen, Helene Rennervik, Caren Cooper, Virginie Lemay, Martin Seville, Dawn Pensack, Jennifer Spor, W. Kevin Ward.*

Your storyteller, Steve

My Creative Journey

Early in 2019, I discovered a set of forgotten short stories I had written thirty years ago. To vary my content on social media, I shared one with my followers. In posting it, the joy of storytelling rekindled in my heart. Readers' responses encouraged me to keep authoring more, prompting me to set a goal of creating an allegory every week to offer leadership tips. The fruit of sowing that seed is this book.

Each story contains a metaphor with a message. You might consider them as parables. I intend to leave you thinking and to challenge you to transform a perception or mindset. This collection exists not to tell you how to be a leader but to fuel purposeful reflection about your leadership.

Message to the Readers

Stories are like paths leading your audience to where you wish them to go. Thank you for coming along on these journeys.

My hope is to guide you to new insights for personal growth as a leader in your workplace, home, and community.

—Steven Lee Sullivan

Why Apples and Oranges?

Leaders create the work conditions in which their people perform. A healthy growth environment spurs individuals to rise to their best, while a toxic environment kills the workers' productivity. As a boss, you might argue your workplace has the vision, feedback, and benefits to keep staff happy. However, the employees may feel surrounded by sand, toiling in the desert. The dryness brings on death as it sucks the life out of them.

When considering your business atmosphere, does it empower people to advance their skills for optimal performance? For many companies, the most valuable asset exists in their human capital. However, they fail to invest adequately in this critical component to turn it into an advantage.

Like apples and oranges, people are biologically similar yet different. In eating an apple or orange, we experience the fruit through distinct texture and taste. Likewise, as we interact with a person, we learn the unique abilities of the individual.

Apples and oranges mature on trees requiring very different climates and specific habitats to flourish. For example, apples need cooler zones often tempered by regional lakes to bloom and prosper, while oranges thrive in humid and hotter temperatures.

Like parents who discover that each of their children has a different love language, requiring unique approaches to nurture and train, you must be a student of your team's needs and meet these for your employees to thrive. Creating the right growth environment for each member provides the habitat for their strengths, values, skills, and personality to produce at a higher level. Like tending an orchard, this effort demands sacrifice by you to achieve exponential results.

This book challenges leaders to expand influence by building solid relationships with direct reports. By serving your people, you gain the authority to make a lasting impact on their lives.

In this collection, the metaphors highlight the emotional intelligence needed to put people first. These images offer creative insights into handling everyday situations and common human interactions. To bring transformation to your team, practice the behaviors emphasized through the allegories.

How to Get the Most from This Book

1) Read one parable a day just for your benefit.

    a. After reading, take five minutes to reflect.

    b. Identify the behaviors observed in the story.

    c. Can you choose a behavior to practice?

    d. What can the metaphorical message teach you? How does it apply to your life and leadership?

    e. Each chapter ends with a question followed by a *Thoughts* section with space to journal an introspection.

2) Spark engagement and discussion with your team and co-workers by reading one in a meeting or an office conversation. Ask:

   a. What do they think of the metaphor?

   b. How do they see you or the team exemplifying the message?

   c. What actions do they recommend for you or the group to live out its meaning?

3) Sponsor or join a discussion group with your peers, book club, or team. A free discussion guide is available. For those interested, see the *Group Discussion* section for more information.

4) When seeking feedback, keep in mind the following techniques:

   a. Listen to hear instead of thinking about how to respond.

   b. Ask clarifying questions to ensure you understand their perspective.

   c. Offer an open invitation to share additional thoughts in the future.

   d. Show gratitude by thanking them for their feedback. If you mention a specific comment you agree with, your appreciation carries more impact.

Apples and Oranges

Rob stopped me after the managers' meeting. "Your team is once again high on the productivity scoreboard. If I only had your group."

"Why? Your unit has talented people," I said.

"My staff won't do the job the way I prefer them to work."

"So, if I understand correctly, you expect your direct reports to function the way you would if you were doing the job?"

"Yes, they all have the same role," Rob said. "My promotion to manager came because of my success in that position. I got results! Employees frustrate me when they fail to do things the way I found successful."

"Are your team members all like you?"

"No, that's the problem. If my staff were clones, they would top every other team in the company!"

"The foundation of our group's accomplishments is that we recognize the diversity of each member's unique strengths and weaknesses, helping one another. As you can see, my people outperform yours."

"What is the secret to your success?" Rob asked.

Reaching into my desk, I brought out an apple and an orange. Taking a bite of one, I said, "This apple tastes sweet and tart. Would you expect the orange to taste like it?"

"Of course not! The fruits are different."

"Like apples and oranges, each person is unique in the way they work. By learning how to leverage an individual's talents, the team performs at a higher level." I continued: "Why do you try to turn your oranges into apples?"

Thoughts

The Tree

The other day our office had a big celebration honoring the salespeople of the year. As I thought of the meeting, I didn't look forward to it. Our team struggled to meet goals. Yet again, I would have to clap and congratulate Joe and his group for their success. Forcing on a smile, I dressed up and vowed next year would be different.

Then I reconsidered, swallowed my pride, and decided to ask Joe for advice, inviting him to lunch to learn his secrets. "What does your team do that mine doesn't? How do you achieve successful results year after year?"

Looking out the window, he pointed to a single tree. "What do you see?"

"A tree whose leaves are turning yellow. How does this help me?"

Joe told me to watch this tree to learn his secret. Despite my pressured questioning, he would say no more on the topic.

As winter turned into spring, the tree blossomed. The leaves grew to flower and produced fruit. Later, when I saw Joe, he asked, "What did you learn from the tree?"

"The normal pattern of life. You aren't helping me! What does this have to do with your success?"

"What do you think made it blossom and bear fruit?"

"The sun, the rain, and the nutrients in the ground. Everybody knows this."

"Nourishment is the key to growth for both trees and people," he said.

Then, facing him head-on, I asked with a profound sense of humility, understanding, and eagerness to learn, "How do you nourish your team?"

Thoughts

The Noise

Sally called. "Can you tell me what to do with Jennie? I can't take her anymore!"

"What is the issue, and how can I help?"

"When I am focusing on work, she comes into my office bent out of shape, complaining, upset, and crying for me to do something. All I hear is negative noise. How did you deal with her when she reported to you? You seemed to manage her okay!"

"Meet me downstairs. Let's go for a walk on Broadway Street." Once on the sidewalk, we walked among the roar of the city until I stopped to arrest her attention further. "Listen to the sounds of the avenue. What do you hear?"

"Besides the cries of uptight people yelling at one another, the honking of horns to get others out of the way, sirens indicating trouble somewhere, and the clang-ing of chaos, what else is there?" Sally asked.

"Pay attention more closely. Can you pick out a melody?"

As we strolled, the faint notes of a street musician played on the corner ahead. "I hear a violin playing," she said.

I nodded approvingly, and when we approached the violinist, he continued to play a beautiful concerto. For several minutes, we stood admiring his skill. "What do you hear now?"

"Wonderful music!" Now focused, she said, "The sounds move my soul and touch my heart."

"What about the turbulence and chaotic noise around us?"

Gazing at the busy avenue, she said, "Oh, I tuned that out as soon as I heard the musical piece."

"This is how I worked with Jennie."

Sally studied my face for understanding. "What do you mean?"

"By listening for what was in her heart and ignoring the noise of her emotions, I could hear the real issue."

"Are you able to hear what matters to your people?"

Thoughts

The Water Lily

L ila pulled me into a meeting room in a panic. "I can't believe this! I just lost the biggest client our company had. What will the CEO think? My job may be on the line."

"Hold it. Take a deep breath and settle your thoughts," I said.

Breathing in slowly, she paused. "Thank you. But how am I ever going to recover from this failed opportunity?"

I began: "Let me tell you of an old tale of lost love by an Indian maiden. When her beloved passed over her for another, she fell into a lake. Drowning in her tears, this virgin took on the form of water lilies. The color white represents her purity, yellow her passion."

Continuing, "Every cycle of the sun brought fresh drama. Each night as the flowers closed, her spirit slept.

In the morning, when the petals unfolded to new light, her heart opened to display her beauty."

Bewildered, Lila said, "I don't understand. What does this story have to do with losing a customer?"

"Lost love can be one of the deepest sorrows we carry when we focus on missed opportunities. In life, difficult events happen. The loss of the account is one more, though painful and disappointing. Now, what are you going to do about it?"

Her mind was too overwhelmed to think straight, so she asked, "What should I do?"

"Look, losses are as much a part of life as gain. There is so much we can't control, but we can control our response to those painful losses. What appears to be a closed door today may be an open door tomorrow, with a new opportunity to show your talent."

"Do you choose to face each day like a water lily opening anew or wallow in the swamp of your despair?"

Thoughts

The Workout

At a lunch meeting with Anne, she shared, "I am pursuing my dreams as an entrepreneur."

Excited for her courage, I responded. "How is it going so far?"

"Very slowly; my progress seems negligible. Despite working hard each day, results are not coming quickly enough, or at least not as fast as I had hoped."

"New entrepreneurs often say similar things."

"Do you have a magic trick to accelerate my business?"

Smiling, I replied, "Ha! No sleight of hand today, only a helpful observation. Come with me."

We walked until reaching a storefront gym full of customers working out on various machines. "Anne, go ahead and carefully take a look at each person exercising. What do you notice?"

She observed the scene for a bit. "Different-sized individuals with diverse fitness levels are lifting weights, doing squats, and running to build stronger bodies. Some appear in excellent shape, while others have a way to go."

"So true! When they came in today, did they expect to leave with a new body from their workout?"

"No, they added weight or repetitions and worked to improve speed, each hoping to advance over time to achieve changes."

"Do you think everyone working out will meet their goals in becoming fit?"

"Not all! Some will stop because they see little improvement from their tireless efforts."

"Exactly! When we can't see progress, it's tough to preserve the inner drive to reach our goal. Building a business requires tenacity to persevere, often without notable headway."

"Will you cease lifting your company weights or keep working until you get to where you desire to be?"

Thoughts

The Cheese

Kristin came into my office, visibly stressed. "What is your secret for staying calm under fire?"

"Kristin, what is bothering you? What happened?"

"My team missed an important deadline, and our failure set back a critical project. Now senior management demands answers."

Taking slices of Swiss cheese, I laid them on my desk. "We all need layers of support to avoid costly mistakes and to operate efficiently. Can we look at your support system to see where holes may have prevented success?"

"Sure," she said.

"Layer one starts with your personal life. So let's check this foundation—care for yourself. How would you grade your self-care? Can you be your best if you are not keeping healthy?"

Kristin became painfully honest. "Not well. Long hours, junk food, anxiety, and little sleep. These threaten my health." Then, shaking her head, she continued, "My New Year's resolution was to become fit. But, after the second week, it fell off my to-do list."

After discussing some realistic next steps she could take to balance those areas, I inquired about organizational gaps contributing to the failure. " Your next layer consists of resource planning. Holes develop when we miscalculate the resources we need to commit. For example, did you account for all the team members you needed?

"No, my group discovered we missed obtaining a database manager from the I.T. team for the critical installation."

"Do you know why the planning failed to recognize the need for this person?"

"During the project plan review, I rushed over it. With a more careful assessment, I would have caught the omission."

 "Okay, we have identified some important things! Now, the last layer of support involves accountability. Tell me about your status report meetings."

She answered sheepishly but transparently, "Scheduling conflicts caused me to skip many progress updates."

With that, I put my finger through the holes in the Swiss cheese to demonstrate her issue. "Can you see how, when the cracks in your support layers line up, an error can pass through? What are you going to adjust to close these gaps?"

Thoughts

The Bill

"Steve, you have to take action regarding Mike," said Jay after a problematic project meeting. "This is the second time he made a mistake, which reflects poorly on you as a manager."

Taking a deep breath, I said, "He is new and learning our processes. When talking with him, I've found him very sharp—full of good ideas to offer. What would you do with an employee like Mike?"

Jay didn't hesitate. "As far as my team, any individual who makes others question my leadership is a problem risk. Removing him from the group would be my first action."

An idea came to me. "Do you have a $20 bill you can show me?"

Reaching into his wallet, he handed me a crisp new $20 note. With a big smile, he said, "You better give it back to me when finished with this little object lesson."

"Why? The tender only amounts to $20, not much when it comes to currency."

"Hey, it's $20 bucks! Who throws away cash?"

In my hand, I crinkled his brand-new bill. "Should I toss it into the trash, now that it's wrinkled?"

"Of course not; it still has value."

Dropping the note on the floor, I ground my shoe on it. The paper crumpled and tore. "Do you still want it?"

Chuckling, Jay said, "Steve, as long as you don't burn it into ashes, yes, I do! The money is still worth $20."

With a smile, I gave back the cash. "No matter what it has gone through, you can still spend it for $20 worth of goods. Jay, I'm just like you; I never throw away an asset. Despite Mike's few mistakes, he remains incredibly valuable to our company. What worth do you place on your team members?"

Thoughts

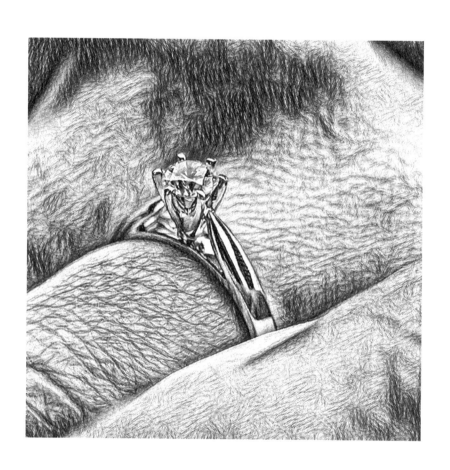

The Flaw

Taking a seat, Jill came into my office in tears and said, "I don't know what to do. I feel so inadequate at my job. Are you sure you want me on your team?"

"Jill, you are a talented person!. Why do you have this impression?"

"My flaws overwhelm me. For starters, I'm absent-minded, anxious, and disorganized. And if that's not enough, I am sure others have noticed other faults. It's so discouraging to know everyone sees me as the weak link on the team."

I noticed a flash of light that caught my attention. Pointing to it, I said, "Where did you find the beautiful diamond ring on your hand?"

As the countenance of her face changed, she said, "Oh! My husband gave it to me for our engagement."

"He has great tastes in gems. Have you ever looked at your diamond up close?"

"Of course! After putting it on, I think I stared at it for hours."

I kept digging further, "What did you see?"

"I could not take my eyes off the stone's radiance, especially shining in the sunlight. When I remember the occasion and the love which captured my heart, excitement and joy fill me again."

"In looking at it closely, did you ever notice something deep inside your gemstone?"

"Oh, yes, there's a carbon speck which is visible to the naked eye. Because I know the blemish is there, I've nicknamed my ring Spot. You're the first person who has inquired about the little black fleck. My friends never mention it."

"Of course, the charcoal particle is a common occurrence found in diamonds. What do your friends see when you show it to them?"

"They gush over the brilliant prism shining through the jewel. They think it is wonderful."

"You are like the diamond. Why focus on your tiny flaws when co-workers stand in awe of your talents?"

Thoughts

Lost

"You look lost. Is everything alright?" I asked, noting my new manager's distressed faced.

Lowering his eyes, Paul said, "Can I be honest?"

"Yes, go right ahead. My job is to support you."

"I worked hard for this promotion, but now as a manager, I feel like an imposter, not knowing what I am doing. My team tells me I am meddling. Delegating tasks often seems harder than performing the work myself. Knowing the right action to take challenges me to the point of frustration. How do you do it? How did you learn to become a good leader?" Paul asked.

Feeling his pain, I replied, "Paul, look, you are not alone. Making mistakes goes with any position. To grow, you have to start somewhere. We all have to be learners for life. Let me inquire. When you are traveling and get lost, do you stop to ask for directions?"

The facial stress eased with a light shrug. "Actually, no. I am always confident in finding my way, maybe too confident. When I stray from the route, I try not to show it, but my wife always knows better. Funny how that works! She hates it when I keep driving."

We both laughed at his admission, as I have been there myself. Our conversation was getting to an important issue. "Let me tell you a secret. Situations come upon me where I do not know what I am doing, but I have a 'superpower.' Would you like to know what it is?"

"Yes, tell me! Tell me! Who wouldn't want this superpower?"

"My superpower is simple. Here it is—humility! Stop and ask for help. When you do, your team (and your wife) might like you better. Nobody expects you to know it all. When we ask good questions and continue learning from others, we will find out what works best for them. That's how we earn respect and move forward. Are you willing to make *The Ask*?"

Thoughts

Two Dogs

Fred approached me. "Can we go for a walk? I need your advice."

"Sure. Meet me downstairs," I said.

As we strolled on the busy street, he started asking about leadership. He noticed my team has almost no departures, except when people leave for promotions. His group has the worst turnover rate in the department, and he considers none of his staff ready for advancement.

"What do you think my secret is?" I asked.

"Your employees like you more than mine like me?"

"Ha! Do you think it matters how much my direct reports like me? Look over and notice those two people walking their dogs. What do you see?"

He noted one woman had a companion dog, watching out for its owner, helping her navigate the crowd and the road to avoid an accident. The other person fought being dragged along by their hound as it pulled and chased scents, causing him to keep constant tension on the leash. We laughed at the poor guy trying to keep his pet in line.

"Do you think these dogs like their caretakers?" I asked.

"I'm sure that they both do! Dogs are man's best friend."

"Then, why does one canine stay with its owner, looking after her wellbeing, while the other pet gets distracted by the smallest things, frustrating its handler?"

"It must relate to their training or lack thereof."

"Right. They say training a service dog takes about two years. Do you think you can get a good guide dog by skipping the instruction?"

"No way!" he said.

"With our teams, the same is true. The more time we spend in training, instruction, and guidance, the more they can contribute increased results and take on greater roles. When they know we care for their best and their professional growth, they remain loyal. All the mentoring, opportunities, additional value given to our staff always end up returning more than we gave. Are you ready to invest the time in your workers to see them perform at a higher level?"

Thoughts

The Apology

Mary knocked softly on my office door. "I need to apologize for upsetting Mrs. Smith."

"Please, come in." I invited.

Moving her white and red cane back and forth, Mary made her way to a chair and sat. "I made a mistake today by calling Mrs. Smith by the incorrect name, causing her to get angry instead of feeling welcomed."

"Yes, Mary, she submitted a complaint to the store, which found its way into my trash can, by the way. You addressed her by her ex-friend's name, the one she went shopping with so many times. None of us knew they had a falling out, much less that using the other name would create an offense."

"But I should have known who she was by her voice."

"Mary, do you know how many glowing compliments come to me? My desk contains a file full of customers' praises regarding you. In greeting people by name as they enter, you amaze them and your co-workers that you can identify them by a simple hello. Acknowledging people in your special way lets them know that they're important to us and brightens their day."

She still couldn't shake the disappointment in herself. "Mrs. Smith doesn't feel that today!"

I quickly put the issue where it belonged. "That is Mrs. Smith's problem, not yours. You're too hard on yourself. Outside my window, an oak tree grows. Some people focus on the lightning scars and the broken limb, seeing only a damaged tree. Mrs. Smith chose to make a big deal of one mistake. Do you know what I see?"

"No, that scarred tree sounds like me," Mary said.

"When I look at that oak, my eyes observe a tree giving life. From the fallen acorns, squirrels scramble to gather food. Up high, birds build nests for their young. The branches extend shade over a bench, where people sit to enjoy their lunches. Kids disappear excitedly behind the thick trunk playing hide and seek. Both animals and humans appreciate the tree being there, even though it is far from perfect."

"Are you going to dwell on your imperfections or let the joy of those who receive life from you inspire you to keep giving of yourself?"

Thoughts

Aged Scotch

My boss called me in for a planning meeting. In reviewing a merger, the leadership team directed us to consider releasing senior workers. The executives prefer to take advantage of the energy and cost savings of the youth.

"Is the decision final, or is it still open for discussion?" I asked.

"The opinion is more of a guide than a mandate. The company plans to move toward promoting the next generation. However, if a compelling reason exists to keep experienced staff over newer employees, we still have the authority to make some choices. What do you think?"

Taking a moment to grasp his words, I responded. "I can see from the bottles on your shelf that you like to sip Scotch."

"Oh, yes. It is my drink of choice, but what does that have to do with this conversation?" He smiled.

"Which would you rather have—alcohol from a bottle of fifty-year-old Scotch or five-year-old Scotch?"

"Most definitely, the best-aged brew I can afford. The older liquor goes down smoothly and pleasingly. Often the younger stuff, though still good, can have a bite. But, like many good things, you get what you pay for."

I returned to the metaphor. "I know that we always need to be open to new ideas from those who haven't been locked into certain patterns of thinking, but have you ever thought your experienced employees are like aged Scotch? Over time they have learned skills, wisdom, knowledge of the business, and streamlined processes that create tremendous value. As a result, they perform as examples for the next generation."

"Tell me, which would you give away, your fifty-year-old Scotch or your five-year-old Scotch?"

Thoughts

The Pearl

I could see Jennie waiting in my office. She looked frustrated and angry. After saying good morning, I asked, "Is there something bothering you?"

"I don't know how to tell you this, but I must quit."

"Did you find an opportunity to do something new and exciting? Jennie, you know you have my support."

"No, no," she interrupted. "Leaving is not what I want to do. My work consists of tasks I enjoy, and in you, I have never had a better boss."

I smiled at the compliment, but her decision was all the more confusing. "As a team member, you have been great, very competent at what you do. I don't want to lose you. What is the matter?"

Looking away, she said, "I guess I don't know how to handle confrontation or disagreements. To everything

I suggest, Joe is contrarian. His commanding presence causes me to shrink back, go silent and not speak up."

Pulling out a seashell, I placed it on my desk. "Do you know how an oyster defends itself from an intruder?"

"No," she said, looking puzzled.

"Have you ever seen a pearl?"

"Of course! My grandmother gave me one of her necklaces made of pearls. They are beautiful, amazing creations."

I kept going with my inquiry. "What causes this wondrous little jewel to form?"

"Something to do with debris," Jennie said.

"No, contrary to popular belief, oysters can expel sand. Instead, the gem forms in defense to an irritant, often an invading parasite. The mollusk seals off the invader with a fluid coating called nacre. Many layers create the growing pearl, surrounding that nuisance with beauty."

"I don't understand how this helps me with my problem."

"When faced with aggravation, do you use your strengths to work through the situation, forming a pearl of personal growth, or do you seek to avoid it and remain the soft clam?"

Thoughts

The Butterfly

Wendy pulled me aside to let me know she was having trouble with a new employee. She found Jim taking a lot of her time as he questioned what to do in every situation.

"Do you give him the answers each time?" I asked.

Squeezing a pen nervously, she admitted, "Yes. New employees require direction, but his constant interruptions keep me from completing my assigned work. I don't have time to hand-hold Jim."

"Wendy, let me ask you, does telling him what to do each time make him less or more dependent on you?"

"Well, my hope is that he will apply the answer to other situations and not come back the next time."

"And how's that working out for you? Does your help create the desired result?"

"No, he just keeps coming back with similar questions for each slightly new change in scenarios."

Reaching into my desk, I pulled out a hand-painted case and gestured. "What do you think of this box?"

"The butterfly on the lid is beautiful! Only the artistic touch of a master painter could create a detailed work like that. But why show me this container?"

"Because this is my answer box. The picture reminds me of a butterfly I tried to help emerge from its cocoon when I was a boy so I could see it sooner. The butterfly failed to take flight and died. Later I learned the struggle to break free from its wrapping is key to strengthening the wings. By me disrupting the process, it couldn't fly."

"I totally get that, but what do you have in the case?"

I leaned forward to whisper my ingenious idea. "When my staff asks for information that I know they can find themselves with a little more effort, I show them this case. Then I proclaim like P. T. Barnum, 'This magical box will reveal all knowledge to your every inquiry. For five dollars, you can see inside to get your answer right now.'"

Wendy quickly pulled a five-dollar bill from her purse. "I've got to see inside to figure out what to do with Jim." Intrigued, she lifted the lid only to see herself looking back at her—a mirror!

"Do you prefer Jim to be dependent or learn to fly?"

Thoughts

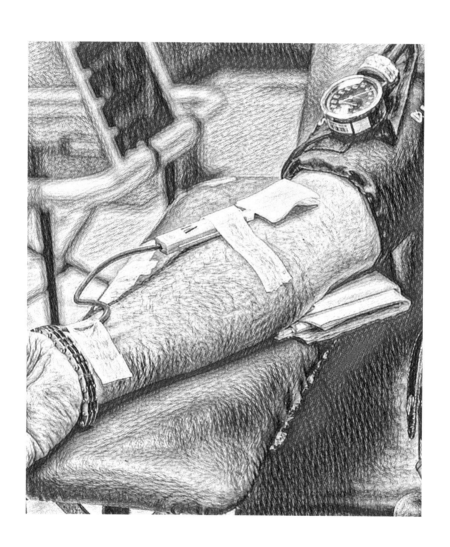

The Blood

Stopping by Vick's work area, I asked how he was adjusting to his new position.

"To be honest, I am discouraged," he said.

"There is a lot to learn. Do you like the role?"

"Oh yes, it's fascinating, and I'm thankful for the job. I'm just dissatisfied with my progress in mastering it."

"Have you talked to Dan? He was assigned to help you succeed."

"That's just it. I am afraid Dan has a problem with me. He seems to avoid me. When I come in, he doesn't even greet me in the hall."

I decided to interject at this point. "Let me speak with Dan to see if I can encourage him to be more helpful."

I called Dan into my office. "Vick could use your assistance in learning the job."

Dan didn't bend: "I can't work with him. He is not my people, not my culture, and I don't understand him."

"Vick is a human being like you and me!"

Still not budging, he persisted: "No, he is not like you or me; he is different."

Noticing a lobby sign, I asked, "Did you see the blood donation event downstairs today?"

"Yes, but I haven't given yet and was planning to go later."

"Good, let's go together."

As we stood in the line, I pointed to the collection area. "Look at all the bags of blood."

"Yes, each one is going to make a difference for an injured person! I am glad our office is participating in the blood drive," Dan said.

"Who do you think contributed all these gifts of life? A variety of people from different backgrounds gave willingly. What if one day you desperately need a transfusion, and it doesn't come from your people?"

"Blood is blood. It does not matter," he said.

"If blood is blood, are we not all human? Are you and Vick not working for the same thing?"

Thoughts

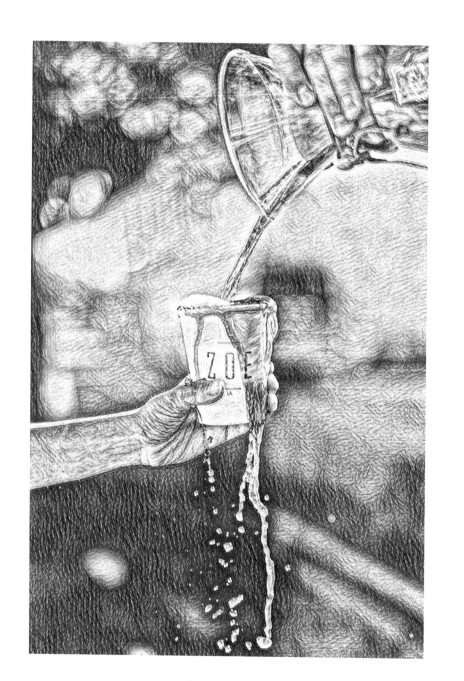

The Cup

When I saw Bob at the meeting, he was sweating and agitated. He looked like a man about to face death. I pulled him aside. "Bob, what is troubling you?"

"I am under the gun to get several projects done. My best never seems to be good enough, and I feel the possibility of losing my job hanging over me like a dark shadow."

"Have you talked to your boss?"

"No. I'm sure I would appear weak in his eyes, and he would just tell me to work weekends. My family already feels neglected with the long hours I am putting in. I hate the husband and parent I have become. Can you help me?"

Surprised, I asked, "How did you get so much on your plate?"

"I was taking on more work to impress my boss while at the same time having a hard time saying no to others when asked for help. Eventually, my work buried me."

"So, in your current state, you are not benefitting anyone right now?"

"Right. I am in chaos, failing to do anything well."

Knowing he must have felt terrible, I said, "Come on, let's get some water and take a breath."

In pouring water into my mug, I purposely looked away. Soon the liquid overflowed, spilling all over the floor.

"Steve, stop filling your cup. It is full. Look at the mess!"

"Uh oh, I got the carpet wet. How did this happen?"

"You didn't pay attention to what you were doing." Bob frowned.

As I started to clean up the spilled water, I said, "When we lose track of what pours into our lives, our cups fill faster than we can handle, and our lives spill everywhere."

"The failure to set boundaries causes us to feel out-of-control. Do you prefer to overflow all over or learn to say no when your cup is full?"

Thoughts

Violet or Gladioli

"**I** did it again," Maggie said.

"Did what?"

"In the managers' meeting, I felt strongly about the direction we should go but didn't speak up."

"I've worked with you long enough to know you have great ideas to offer. So, why do you sit quietly in the meetings?"

"I go in prepared, but then Fred speaks out quickly and has everybody agreeing with him before I can say a word otherwise. So I shrink back."

"Is he the real reason?"

"Not really. If I'm honest, I fear being wrong and thought of as incompetent," Maggie admitted.

"Let's go for a walk to discuss this further." Leaving the building, we hiked a path near the office into a forest.

"See what flowers you can find a little way into the shaded woods?"

She walked over to brush aside some foliage and smiled. "Oh, nice! Some pretty little violets are hiding among the other plants."

I wanted her to notice something else. "Okay, now turn and view the meadow. What do you see?"

"A beautiful landscape full of gladioli. The flowers stand straight and tall in the glory of their colors."

Taking a moment to enjoy the scene, I said, "A poet once wrote about those violets: 'Here and there, by the thorny underwood a shrinking violet.'"

I continued with a contrast. "On the other hand, ancient Roman gladiators wore gladioli when entering the arena. The flowers symbolize a sword for strength and power."

"Maggie, what do you aspire to be? A shrinking violet or a mighty gladiolus?"

Thoughts

The House

While spending time with a friend from Down Under discussing life in America and Australia, he brought up the proliferation of self-help books and resources in the USA. "Why do you spend so much time talking about wellbeing? When you tell people you must have self-love, I think you Yanks are nuts."

"How do you Aussies consider personal growth?"

"We know what we need to know to survive."

"So, in your view, strength matters only in your actions?"

"Bloody oath." Patrick bragged. "Now, tell me I am wrong."

"Do you live in a house?" I asked.

"What, do you think I shelter in the bush, mate? I own a house like yours!"

"Sometimes, you make me wonder," I jabbed in good fun. "What is the most important thing in your house?"

"My family!"

"Wouldn't you do anything to protect and provide for them?" I asked.

"You know I would. My wife and children are my pride and joy. Without them, I would lose my way."

Developing my point, I asked, "Okay, so what would happen if you left holes in your roof or a shattered window unfixed?"

"If I allowed my house to stay damaged, cold and rain would make it miserable, and the water would ruin the structure. Straight away, I would fix any issue to care for my family."

"So, you would act out of self-preservation to repair your house?" I smiled.

"You got me, mate."

"As human beings, we all have blind spots, weaknesses, and holes in our dignity, allowing in doubts, criticism, and loathing. We need to address these shortcomings with intentional learning to protect our strength and help others. Whether you call it personal growth, self-help, or self-love, we cannot afford to stagnate."

"What do you do when you need to mend yourself?"

Thoughts

The Redwood

A new employee joined our team and was having diffi-culty learning his new role. To help him, I called Joe into my office. "Could you spend more time helping our new team member understand the work?"

"Can't you find someone else to help him? Besides, I tried, and he doesn't get it. I have no more time for him."

"Are you suggesting we leave him to flounder?"

Joe bristled, "I think he needs to either sink or swim in learning the job."

"Do you care if he succeeds or not?"

"What I care about are my projects! I am focused on making sure I succeed."

I asked one last question. "Have you ever heard of heart rot in trees?"

"No."

"When a tree develops heart rot, it decays from the inside out until it dies. The tree's susceptibility to heart rot lies with how the sap ring builds the trunk's core. For example, in a redwood tree, the inner cells help the new cells by absorbing the external toxins into the sap. On the other hand, in a birch tree, the cells ignore the contaminants. Which tree do you think becomes more resistant to decay?"

Joe responded thoughtfully, "The redwoods—I'm sure because they live for such a long time."

"Yes, by the sap ring taking on the toxins, it gives the tree's core a good defense against the fungus that otherwise leads to heart rot. Unfortunately, the sap ring in the birch lacks the substances to fight off the decay."

"Like a redwood, we can carry our co-workers' burdens. In so doing, we build resistance to the forces that bring internal destruction to an entire team."

"What do you choose to be in how you relate to your staff, a redwood or a birch?"

Thoughts

The Trash

Kevin stormed into my office. "Did you see the trash dumped all over my desk? My area is a total mess. When I find out who did this, I'll fire him!"

"Sit down," I said. "I emptied the debris on your counter."

Looking stunned, he demanded. "Why did you do that?"

"Yesterday, you mentioned how your team couldn't work together, and you asked me if I could deal with the situation. So I dumped the litter as an object lesson. Have you asked yourself why your staff is having difficulties?"

"It's because they cannot agree on issues, and they disrespect one another."

"That wasn't my question. Have you considered your role in the team's behavior?"

"What? Do you think it is my fault?" He went from angry to being defensive.

"How did you respond when finding rubbish in your room?"

"I was ticked! My anger boiled over, I saw red, and I couldn't tackle the projects I needed to do."

"Did you notice those wadded papers were your creations?"

"No, but why does that matter? Those documents were mistakes, drafts, or otherwise useless to me."

I probed further. "Like those reports you created, you generate attitudes toward others that get reproduced in the group. Every time you let loose on your team, you pour your garbage on them. When you don't listen or respect their opinions, you convey they have little value to give. They are just acting out your example."

"Wow, you don't hold back! I hear you saying that to turn this around, I must improve how I interact with my group."

"Exactly. If you want to see change, start with you. Face how your actions influence your employees. Take accountability for the dysfunction, which comes from the top down."

"Will you clean up the mayhem beginning with you?"

Thoughts

Your Bond

"With your tribe, job, and the community demanding your time, how do you keep a balance and avoid chaos?" Fred asked.

I turned the question around to him: "Are you clear about your priorities?"

"Yes, I know family, work, society. The difficulty is handling the never-ending requests."

"Fred, do you ever say, No?"

"When so many people need extra hands for good causes, I find it difficult not to pitch in."

"So you feel overwhelmed, overcommitted, and then more important things slip, am I right?"

"Exactly," Fred said. "Then I feel terrible when I miss a commitment to people who were counting on me."

"… And the stress level builds," I said.

"Yes, you got that right! It's exhausting."

Reaching into my pocket, I pulled out a rock. "Have you seen a stone like this before?"

"I don't think so. The sky blue stripes are unique."

"It's called a blue lace agate, and the color stands for trust. As it combines with the gray quartz, the gem symbolizes a person's communications, meaning 'my word is my bond.'"

Continuing, I explained, "To remind me of the pledge I've given to others, I carry it in my pocket. Before making a new commitment, I grasp it in my fist. As I think of my closed hand, my thoughts recall my promises to my wife and family. Next, I remember my agreement to fulfill my responsibilities to this company. Only after these do I take stock of my pledges to assist others in the community or consider additional commitments."

I ended with one last point. "This stone reminds me to let my 'yes' be 'yes,' and my 'no' be 'no.' There will always be people who want my help."

"What can you use as a reminder of your commitments to assure a good self-check before taking on more?"

Thoughts

The Seed

"Have you ever struggled to know what to do?" asked my CEO friend.

"Come on! As the leader of a company, you didn't get there by not knowing what to do. So what is troubling you?"

"I feel like I need a new challenge. My organization is great, but I've led it so long it is hard to see myself doing something else. Besides, I wouldn't know what else to do."

"If you could do anything, what would you like to do?"

"Give back to the community and not just money. I want to get my hands dirty and make a difference in the world."

"Tell me about your staff. Have you developed capable people to take over the corporate operations?"

"Oh yes, if I were willing to let go, my staff could step in to keep the business running smoothly. They need very little from me now."

"Are you having conversations with them about your desire to step back from work?"

That's when he finally admitted, "I'm afraid to talk to them before I am ready to leave."

I was blunt. "When you want to make the transition, come back to me."

"But wait, how can I let go and become something entirely new?"

Taking a bite out of my apple, I pulled out a seed from the core. "Do you know how this grows into a tree?"

"First, you have to plant it in the ground," he replied.

"What happens to it in the soil?"

"If conditions are right, it sprouts as a sapling."

Then I got to the bottom line: "For the kernel to change into a flourishing, fruitful tree, it first has to die to what it is to take on a new form. Are you willing to perish to the current you to transform into a bold new you?"

Thoughts

The Sea

"Why does my team grade me so hard?" Martin asked.

I replied, "What did your latest employee satisfaction scores tell you?"

"Their low grades make me feel underappreciated for what I do for them."

Needing to know more, I asked, "What special things have you done for them?"

"When deciding on what time to work, they can start anywhere between 7-9 AM and leave at the right time. Then, when they perform a good job, I give them lunch rewards, and on my desk, I have sweets for them."

Stopping him, I said, "Hold it. The company's policy lets staff choose their hours. How many meal cards have you given away in the last year? How fast does your candy bowl empty?"

"In the last twelve months, I passed out maybe three free lunches, and my goodies container goes untouched. They seem afraid to visit my office. Why do they fear me?"

"Can you see the free lunches and candy are not motivating them? Look out the window," I suggested. "How is the sea today?"

"Big waves are pounding the beach. I see a terrible storm looming on the horizon."

"Does that darkness encourage you to walk on the shore?"

"No." He turned to watch the wind blow and the swells roll in.

I wanted him to think more deeply. "When the water calms down, what can you see?"

"The clarity of the ocean allows you to see fish swimming among those beautiful coral reefs. On those days, I love to stroll on the beach."

"When your team sees you stressed, venting anger toward them, do they feel safe around you? What do you think they sense in you in those moments? Do they see the beauty of a calm sea inviting them for a walk, or do they feel the pounding of your waves and take shelter?"

Thoughts

The Big Fish

"Steve, regarding the presentation, I can't give it, " Fred said.

"Why not?"

"When I try to speak before an audience, I fail. At my sixth-grade play, you should have seen me. I got on stage and froze. I forgot my lines and ran off the set in tears. So embarrassed with all the kids laughing at me, I didn't want to return to school."

"That was years ago when you were a child! You're such an expert on this subject; you could give the talk in your sleep now."

"Steve, please, can't you find someone else to address our customer group?"

Not answering, I motioned for Fred to follow me. At the local marine aquarium, we visited a particular experiment.

As we approached a large tank containing freshwater creatures, I pointed, "What do you see?"

"A large Northern Pike on one side of the aquarium and baitfish on the other side."

"Why doesn't the big one eat the smaller ones?"

"There is a glass divider between the two, keeping them apart."

"Now watch. The scientists are going to remove the barrier. You can guess what will happen, right?"

"Sure! The pike will make a quick meal of the others."

Although the attendants had not fed the predator in two weeks, the large fish completely ignored the tiny ones after they removed the glass divider. Amazingly, even as the small ones swam close, the hungry pike treated the little fish as if they weren't there.

Fred asked with astonishment, "Why doesn't the hungry one attack the feeder fish?"

"Here's what the marine biologists learned. When the big fish tried earlier, it butted into the glass wall. After several attempts to catch the baitfish, the predator became conditioned to believe it couldn't grab them."

Looking at Fred, I asked, "Have you convinced yourself not to try again because of past failure?"

Thoughts

The Caterpillar

heard a tapping at my door. "May I come in and speak with you?" Anna asked.

"Yes, what can I do for you?"

"There is something I need to get off my chest." With a sigh, she said, "My job makes me feel stuck spinning my wheels, doing the same thing each day. In my heart, I want to make a difference, where people see more in me."

"What would you like to do to make a difference?"

"I'm not sure, with my limited skills. If I left this job, I am not sure what I would pursue. What advice do you have?"

Pointing to a mesh container, I said, "What do you see in the cage?"

"A tree branch with some partially eaten leaves. Why would you keep this in your office?"

"Look closer, Anna. Do you see anything else in there?"

Walking around the enclosure, she said, "Oh, just behind a leaf, I see a cocoon."

"What made it, and what comes out of it?"

"Everyone knows a caterpillar spins the chrysalis. In time a butterfly emerges with beautiful wings. I'd love to be, as the Spanish say, a mariposa."

I pressed further. "How does an ugly, hairy worm turn into a colorful winged creature?"

"I don't know. Some kind of miracle, I guess."

"Believe it or not, the larva goes through a process where it actually dissolves to give life to the butterfly. Are you willing to let your current self-beliefs dissolve into something new to become amazing?"

Thoughts

The Telephone

"For some reason, my messages don't seem to be reaching people. I've got to communicate more effectively. Do you have any suggestions?" Don asked.

"Tell me about your communications. Are you telling them what you think they need to know?"

"Yes, and I emphasize the importance of what I'm saying."

I turned the question around to make a point: "How often do you listen to the basic messages of others telling you what they think you should know?"

The light started going on. "Right, not so much. Those statements get tuned out."

"Do you remember as kids playing telephone with two cans and a string?"

"You're showing your age, my friend," Don said, teasing. "Growing up, my friends and I saw our parents using cell phones, so we used blocks as phones.

Smiling, I said, "Thank you for reminding me I grew up in the last century. How well did you hear your friend?"

"Through the play phones, we always believed the other person was listening, but once outside of voice range, we heard nothing at all, and the game came to an end."

"Let me ask you, Don, do you think your words are something you imagine others hear, like playing telephone?"

"I get it. Communication is only as good as what others perceive, not what I think I'm saying. How can I learn to say things better?"

"Do you craft your communication to meet your audience's objectives and build bridges to them?"

"Hmm. I have not really considered that."

"What do you think they want to hear from you to do their work well?"

"Good question. Maybe, I should ask the team."

"Which would you rather use? Intentional communications that meet real needs, or two cans and a string to broadcast your messages?"

Thoughts

The Rock

In Char's voice, I could hear the sadness. "Sir, I need to talk to you, but I am not sure how to tell you."

I could tell this would be serious, so I thought escaping the office to the nearby path might help her get out what she needed to express. "Let's go for a walk," I said.

As we strolled along the lake, I didn't speak, waiting for Char to share what was troubling her. She began, "I know I have not been at my top performance lately." She grew even quieter. On her face flowed tears, shame, and a struggle to find the words.

Finally, she spilled it out. "My fiancé, now my ex-fiancé, crushed my heart. The most precious gift I could give him, he trashed, making it worse by leaving me for a close friend. Can you see why I am unable to focus on work?"

"I am sorry to hear about your hurt. Your situation must be hard to admit, and I thank you for trusting me. What can I do to help?"

She blurted through the pain, "Pull out my heart so I can refocus and get back to doing my job!"

Standing on the path, I pointed to a big rock, "Is this a fair picture of how you feel?"

"Maybe! I wish my soul could be that hard. Then the pain would go away."

"Besides the hardness, what else do you see?"

"An unmovable object."

"Look again at the boulder and describe it to me."

She studied it again and said, "The surface has several cracks. An amazing flower is growing out of one crack. From one of the other openings springs a small tree, and in another is a clump of grass."

"Yes, even from a rock comes new life. Do you prefer to feel like the hard, immovable boulder or embrace new life out of the pain?"

Thoughts

The Rowboats

As we talked about the weekend, Dave and I made plans to escape to our favorite fishing spot on the river. As busy leaders under heavy pressure to produce, we looked forward to an easy day sitting by the water, smelling the fresh forest air, and leaving behind our burdens.

After putting out our poles, we settled in peace to observe our lines. The river's gentle flow calmed us until Dave broke the quiet. "Steve, how do you get your employees to perform so well?"

"I'm surprised by the question. You hire talented people. Aren't they performing as you expected?"

"I am always having to tell them what to do, correcting their work, or getting on their case for making bad choices. My blood pressure rises just watching them!"

"Do you want to problem-solve or relax today?"

Smiling, he turned back to fishing.

Into view came two rowboats on the river. One navigated past the rocks while one kept crashing into them, almost capsizing. Both boats had people rowing with their backs facing downstream, and each crew relied on a navigator to keep them off the boulders.

"Do you see the guy running along the bank yelling instructions to the rowboat having trouble?" I asked.

It took a moment for David to stop laughing. "Too funny! He is getting angry at the rowers for hitting the rocks as he runs down the shore shouting. I wish I had a camera when he tripped over deadwood on the sand and fell into the water."

"Which navigator can see the submerged boulders better and guide his group around the dangers?"

"The one sitting in the rowboat obviously can see a lot better than the guy on the shore."

"Dave, do you want to know how to improve your team's performance?"

"Yes, anything to lessen my stress."

"The key is whether you chase after your team along the shore or get into the boat with them. Which will you do?"

Thoughts

The Web

Rachel burst into my office. "There is no way I will speak to Joe again!"

Turning from my work, I let out a breath. "What on earth happened between you?"

"At the status meeting, he humiliated me!"

"Are you sure he meant to hurt you? Together you have been the most innovative pair on my team. Surely you don't want that collaboration to end?"

"After how he made me feel today, I am not talking to him."

"I have seen the two of you talking in the parking lot for hours after a business day. As designers, you weave a web of creative ideas, feeding off each other's input."

"Well, I don't see us working together in the future," she insisted.

"Rachel, do you know much about spiders?"

"All I know is that I hate them."

"I want you to see something important. An arachnid's home is a marvelous feat of engineering. The strands all lead to the center of the overall design with incredible consistency."

To help her see the application, I said, "Creative conversations are like a spider's web. As you brainstorm ideas, thoughts build in many directions until they converge at a point of inspiration or revelation. It's magical the way you two collaborate. Do you really wish to end those exchanges?"

Her countenance calmed as she acknowledged, "Those discussions were the best part of working with him."

"A spider's net is a fragile thing, broken by the wrong touch. To catch its next meal, a spider must recreate it daily."

Then I applied the metaphor to people: "With people, we may have to repair our relationships to work together. It's not always easy, but it is so worth it. The productivity you and Joe have is worth it! Are you willing to talk things over with Joe to rebuild your creative web?"

Thoughts

The Tapestry

"**D**o you ever think about your legacy—wonder if you've made a difference in the world?" Chris asked.

Her question made me think. "Sometimes. I desire to leave an example for others to follow. What about you?"

"Sure! As I get older, I question what people will remember and if my life mattered."

"Chris, you have achieved great business success," I said, "Do you want future generations to recognize you for your accomplishments? Like Rockefeller, Carnegie, or Morgan? Of course, some referred to them as 'Robber Barons' and others as 'Captains of Industry.' The perspective depends on whether you recall their cut-throat practices or their philanthropy to the community."

"No," Chris said. "When my life is over, I aspire to leave this place a better world than it was when I came into it."

"Come with me to the Museum of Textiles. There is an exhibit I would like you to see."

As we walked around the galley, Chris found some weavings hanging from the middle of the room. "Why did they hang these rugs like this?"

"The curators hung them away from the wall so we could see both sides of the fabric," I explained.

Chris noticed, "It's so interesting. On one side, you see loose threads tied in all different directions, but on the other side, there's this beautiful work of art."

"Kind of like us," I said. "When we see what is behind us, the failures and achievements make our lives appear to be a mess. But outwardly, people view us like a majestic tapestry."

"The question is, what are we weaving in our life? Are we using threads of selfishness to create a burlap bag, or are we masterfully weaving love to help others fulfill their beautiful and creative purposes?"

Thoughts

The Ship

S ally poked her head into my office. "Have you talked to Fred today? If not outright angry, he looks lost and discouraged."

"How long has he been in a bad mood?" I asked.

"Several members of my team have come to me this week complaining about Fred's harsh words and snide remarks. None want to work with or be around him."

"I have a good idea of what is causing these emotional responses. Let me talk to Fred."

Inviting him to speak with me, I said, "Fred, people have noticed your sour mood around the office. What is burning inside you?"

With a sigh, he said, "I know I haven't been the best toward people. Since I did not get the promotion, I am so frustrated and find myself thinking, *I didn't get it because I am not good enough or as likable as Dave.*"

"So, in your hurt and anger, you've started projecting negativity onto your co-workers? Will beating yourself or others with your words help ease your pain?"

Fred began to see what his reaction was doing to others. "I'm so sorry. Shall I apologize to the team? Acting out is not good for anyone. Help me to change?"

Reaching into my desk, I pulled out a model schooner. "Do you know what steers a ship?"

"The rudder?" Fred answered.

"Yes. Isn't it amazing that one of the smallest parts of the boat has the power to direct it? Your words are like a wheel directing your thoughts by what you say. If what you say to yourself and those around you remains unchecked, your self-talk runs with the storms of life like a rudderless yacht, crashing on the rocks of negativity. The other option is to control our tongue to land at a healthy place. Where do you want to direct your words?"

Thoughts

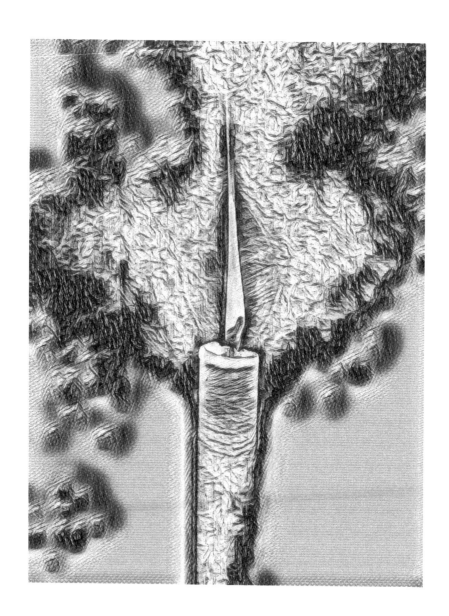

The Candle

"**C**an I speak with you?" Jordan asked. "My employee satisfaction scores are going to hold me back from getting a promotion. Last year my results were low, and they are down again this period. Please, if I am ever to move into higher levels of leadership, I need help."

"What did the survey ratings and comments indicate?" I asked, probing for more to go on.

"Several rated morale as poor. They also complained about ineffective communications and my failure to provide feedback."

"Do you think their assessments have merit?"

Obviously stung by the survey, he replied, "In our regular team meetings, they can ask questions. When there is company news, I am good about passing it along in an email. What more do they expect?"

Taking a candle from the shelf, I placed it in front of him. "If I turn off the lights, will I be able to lead you through the office with this unlit wax stick?"

Jordan scoffed: "No, we would stumble around in the dark like blind men."

Lighting a match, I held it up. "What if I put fire to the wick?"

"With a single candle, we wouldn't see very far, but if I stay close to you, I can follow you."

"Very true. A sole candle is good only for settings where people are near enough to see where the flame shines. As a leader, we are no more than one candle in the corporation. Jordan, if our team fails to see us, we are no better than an unlit wick. To guide our teams, we must do so on a visible level. Leadership means relating in a very personal way."

"Are you willing to use your light to lead one person at a time?"

Thoughts

The Lamp

Coming into my office, Doug took a seat in front of me. "You are always pulling stuff out of your desk. Do you have a magic lamp I could use to rub away my job frustrations?"

Grinning from ear to ear, I said, "This is your lucky day!" Taking out an object, I said, "Behold, out of my drawer appears an old oil lamp worthy of Aladdin."

"Are you kidding me?" he said incredulously." Is there anything you don't have in your workspace?"

"Umm, bags of money! Now, tell me what bothers you."

Doug mockingly rubbed the magic oil lamp but spoke seriously, "I wish to work at something else, and I wish to busy myself with something I love, and I wish I knew what to do."

Stopping him, I said, "Wait, wait! Those are three wishes. I have to limit you there."

"What should I do? In my current situation, I feel stuck."

"Do you know what your strengths are? Have you identified your values, what you enjoy doing, and how your personality fits with a role?"

Shaking his head, he said, "I guess I am too busy focusing on what I don't like to stop and think about what I do like."

"Think about the poor guy caught in the lamp. Do you think this genie feels trapped? Do you think he would like to do something different? Like, be a real person, unlimited by his past choices? If you had the power, would you free him to live a new life?"

Doug stared blankly, "And exactly what does the genie's situation have to do with mine?"

"The genie is you, Doug. You are stuck, and you haven't paused long enough to evaluate your uniqueness and how to leverage it to bring out your best. Will you stay trapped or release yourself to find what you desire?"

Thoughts

Group Discussion

When people come together to share thoughts, they encourage further insights and growth. To participate in group discussions, consider the following options:

1. If you want to facilitate a group conversation with your team, you can find a free discussion guide at bit. ly/AODiscussionGuide

2. If you would like to participate in an online group, see the following for more information at ConfidenceRediscovered.com

Photo Credits

Thank you to the photographers who shared their work through the public domain. I used a sketching tool to create the published versions in this book.

Apples and Oranges Photo by Sarah Gualtieri on Unsplash
The Tree Photo by Aaron Burden on Unsplash
The Noise Photo by Kenny Luo on Unsplash
The Water Lily Photo by Arun Devan on Unsplash
The Workout Photo by Damir Spanic on Unsplash
The Cheese Photo by NastyaSensei on Pexels
The Bill Photo by Annette Fischer on Unsplash
The Flaw Photo by Simon John-McHaffie on Unsplash
Lost Photo by Fabrizio Conti on Unsplash

Two Dogs Licensed from Dreamstime File ID:
164226375

The Apology Photo by Jeremy Bishop on Unsplash

Aged Scotch Photo by Josh Appel on Unsplash

The Pearl Licensed from Dreamstime File ID:
135831309

The Butterfly Photo by David Clode on Unsplash

The Blood Photo by LuAnn Hunt on Unsplash

The Cup Photo by Tyler Nix on Unsplash

Violet or Gladioli (violet) Photo by Irina Iriser (gladioli)
Photo by Steve Doig on Unsplash

The House Photo by Steven Sullivan

The Redwood Photo by Steven Sullivan

The Trash Photo by Steve A Johnson on Pixabay

Your Bond Photo by Cytonn Photography on Unsplash

The Seed Photo by Jose Hernandez-Uribe on Unsplash

The Sea Photo by Marcus Woodbridge on Unsplash

The Big Fish Photo by Yaoqi LAI on Unsplash

The Caterpillar Photo by Suzanne D. Williams on
Unsplash

The Telephone Licensed from Dreamstime File ID:
35547951

The Rock Photo by Char Aukland

The Rowboats Photo by Matthew Buchanan on
Unsplash

The Web Photo by John Doyle on Unsplash

The Tapestry Photo by Sophie Vinetlouis on Unsplash

The Ship Photo by Joseph Barrientos on Unsplash

The Candle Photo by Marc Ignacio on Unsplash

The Lamp Photo by Kerim Sarigul from Pixabay

About the Author

Writer, storyteller, speaker, and coach Steve Sullivan enjoys using creative insights to bring value to his clients, audiences, and followers. In working with tech startups, insurance, and healthcare companies, his leadership experience spans more than three decades, including serving as Chief Information Security Officer.

At age twenty-five, Steve was diagnosed with leukemia (AML). Doctors told him he had less than a five percent chance of living more than a year. He beat the disease and has spent his career working with all levels of personnel in business, from board members, c-suite, directors, managers, staff, and volunteers.

Steve is a graduate of Wheaton College and a YouMap® Certified Coach. As a coach, he takes a holistic approach to help leaders discover their unique value.

Passionate about encouraging people, Steve has volunteered on many service projects in Mexico, Honduras, and Nepal. As part of his personal mission, he has visited inmates at six prisons in the U.S. and Honduras.

He enjoys sailing, fishing, and canoeing on trips into the Boundary Waters Canoe Area (BWCA).

Steve welcomes engagement through social media and invites you to follow him on LinkedIn at linkedin.com/in/steve-sullivan-it.

Need a Speaker or Coach

Are you looking for a fresh voice for your live or virtual conference, or would you like to have Steve on your podcast?

Most Requested Topics

- **Resiliency**—How to have nine lives and land on your feet

- **Power of Words**—How to speak life into others

- **Leadership**—What surviving cancer taught me about leadership

- **Storytelling**—How to tell your story to make an impact

Steve Sullivan is an experienced leadership coach who equips leaders and teams to succeed:

- Transform your staff into great team leaders.
- Learn how to leverage your strengths and build productive teams.
- Strengthen your employees' confidence to achieve their goals.

To work with Steve, visit <u>ConfidenceRediscovered.com</u> or connect with him on LinkedIn: linkedin.com/in/steve-sullivan-it.

CPSIA information can be obtained
at www.ICGtesting.com
Printed in the USA
BVHW041717201021
619402BV00007B/70